APR 08 2015

S0-DGK-032

Making Circle Graphs

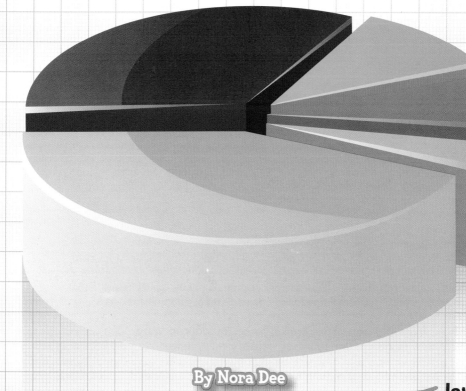

By Nora Dee

 Gareth Stevens
PUBLISHING

PUBLIC LIBRARY SAN MATEO, CALIFORNIA

[leveled reader] math

Please visit our website, www.garethstevens.com. For a free color catalog of all our high-quality books, call toll free 1-800-542-2595 or fax 1-877-542-2596.

Library of Congress Cataloging-in-Publication Data

Dee, Nora.
Making circle graphs / by Nora Dee.
   p. cm. — (Graph it!)
Includes index.
ISBN 978-1-4824-0830-0 (pbk.)
ISBN 978-1-4824-0831-7 (6-pack)
ISBN 978-1-4824-0829-4 (library binding)
1. Graphic methods — Juvenile literature. 2. Mathematics — Charts, diagrams, etc. — Juvenile literature. 3. Mathematical statistics — Graphic methods — Juvenile literature. I. Title.
QA40.5 D44 2015
510—d23

Published in 2015 by
Gareth Stevens Publishing
111 East 14th Street, Suite 349
New York, NY 10003

Copyright © 2015 Gareth Stevens Publishing

Designer: Katelyn E. Reynolds
Editor: Therese Shea

Photo credits: Cover, pp. 1–24 (background texture) ctrlaplus/Shutterstock.com; cover, pp. 1, 7, 9, 11, 13, 17, 19, 21 (circle graph elements) Colorlife/Shutterstock.com; p. 5 (main) Aleksandr Bryliaev/Shutterstock.com; p. 5 (inset) Chuck Place/iStock/ Thinkstock.com; p. 17 (photo) Comstock Images/Stockbyte/Thinkstock.com.

All rights reserved. No part of this book may be reproduced in any form without permission in writing from the publisher, except by a reviewer.

Printed in the United States of America

CPSIA compliance information: Batch #CS15GS: For further information contact Gareth Stevens, New York, New York at 1-800-542-2595.

Contents

Boldface words appear in the glossary.

Pie Pieces

Graphs help us **compare** facts. In a circle graph, the circle **represents** a whole set. Each piece of the circle is a part of the whole set. The parts look like pie pieces. That's why circle graphs are sometimes called pie graphs or pie charts.

In this circle graph, the circle represents a whole class. One piece of the circle represents one student. Bigger pieces mean a larger part, or fraction, of the set. Smaller pieces mean a smaller fraction of the set.

Our Class

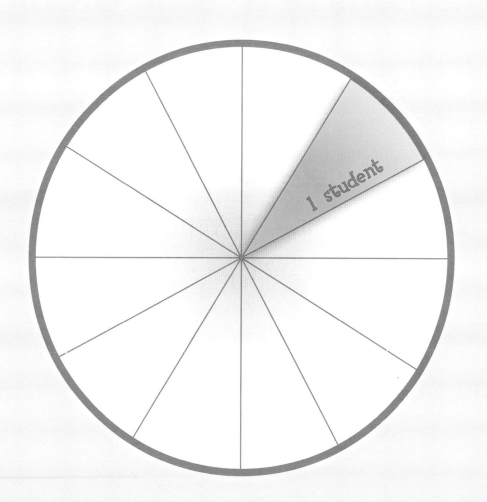

1 student

The Parts of a Circle Graph

All circle graphs have certain parts. A circle graph's title tells you what the graph is about. Look at this graph. What is the title: "In the Fish Tank" or "Red Goldfish"? Check your answer on page 22.

In the Fish Tank

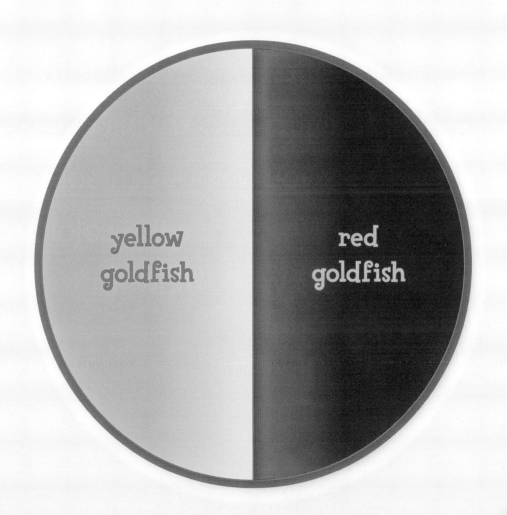

yellow goldfish

red goldfish

The pieces of a circle graph are often different colors. In this graph, a **label** tells you what each color represents. What does the color red stand for? Which flower grows in $\frac{1}{2}$ of the garden?

Flowers in the Garden

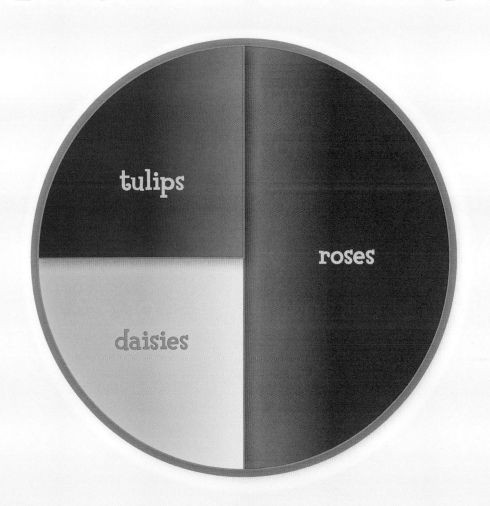

Some circle graphs don't have labels. They have a **key** instead. Look at this graph and key. What fraction of the class did homework last night, $\frac{1}{4}$ or $\frac{1}{2}$?

What Did the Class Do Last Night?

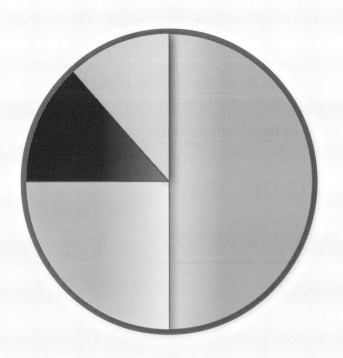

- ☐ homework
- ☐ watched TV
- ■ played games
- ☐ played sports

Graphing with Sports

Now you know a bit about circle graphs. Let's try making one. Imagine asking six friends their favorite sport. Their answers are in the table on the next page. How many friends like basketball best?

sport	How many friends like it best?
baseball	**2**
soccer	1
Karate	1
basketball	2

Now, let's make a circle graph. First, draw a circle on paper. Next, **divide** the circle into six equal parts, one for each friend. Make a key, and use a different color for each sport. Your graph should look a bit like the one here.

baseball

soccer

karate

basketball

17

Color two circle pieces red for the friends who like baseball best. Color one piece yellow for the friend who likes soccer. Color one piece green for the friend who likes karate. Color two pieces blue for the friends who like basketball.

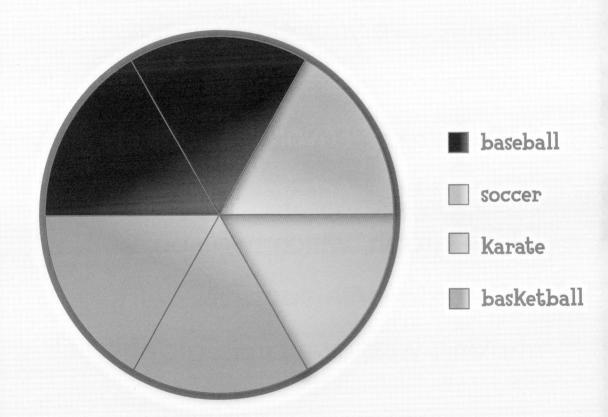

baseball

soccer

Karate

basketball

19

Finally, give your circle graph a title to tell others what it's about. "My Friends' Favorite Sports" is a good title. According to your circle graph, which two sports tied for favorite sport? Now try making your own circle graph!

My Friends' Favorite Sports

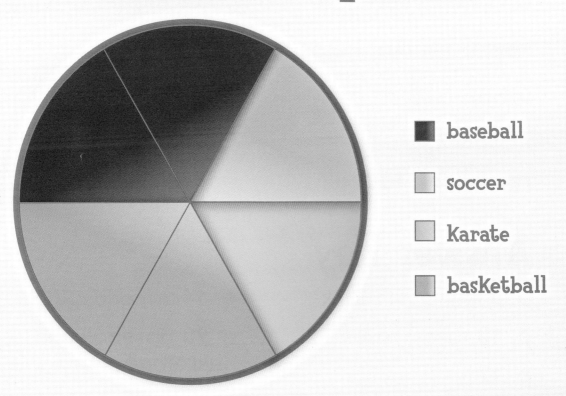

- baseball
- soccer
- karate
- basketball

Glossary

compare: to find what is the same and what is different about two or more things

divide: to separate into two or more parts

key: a list that helps explain a graph or map

label: a word or words used to describe something

represent: to stand for

Answer Key

p. 8 In the Fish Tank

p. 10 roses, roses

p. 12 $\frac{1}{2}$

p. 14 2 friends

p. 20 baseball and basketball

For More Information

Books

Bodach, Vijaya. *Pie Graphs*. Mankato, MN: Capstone Press, 2008.

Cocca, Lisa Colozza. *Pie Graphs*. Ann Arbor, MI: Cherry Lake Publishing, 2013.

Piddock, Claire. *Line, Bar, and Circle Graphs*. New York, NY: Crabtree, 2010.

Websites

Circle Graphs and Pie Charts
www.mathplayground.com/piechart.html
Make your own online circle graphs, also known as pie graphs or pie charts.

Pie Chart
www.mathsisfun.com/data/pie-charts.html
Read more about this kind of graph.

Publisher's note to educators and parents: Our editors have carefully reviewed these websites to ensure that they are suitable for students. Many websites change frequently, however, and we cannot guarantee that a site's future contents will continue to meet our high standards of quality and educational value. Be advised that students should be closely supervised whenever they access the Internet.

Index